CW00548868

HEREFORD IN 50 BUILDINGS

DEREK FOXTON & RON SHOESMITH

AMBERLEY

First published 2019

Amberley Publishing, The Hill, Stroud
Gloucestershire GL5 4EP

www.amberley-books.com

Copyright © Derek Foxton & Ron Shoesmith, 2019

The right of Derek Foxton & Ron Shoesmith to be identified as the Authors of this work has been
asserted in accordance with the Copyrights, Designs and Patents Act 1988.

Map contains Ordnance Survey data © Crown copyright and database right [2019]

All rights reserved. No part of this book may be reprinted or reproduced or utilised in any form or
by any electronic, mechanical or other means, now known or hereafter invented, including
photocopying and recording, or in any information storage or retrieval system, without the
permission in writing from the Publishers.

British Library Cataloguing in Publication Data.
A catalogue record for this book is available from the British Library.

ISBN 978 1 4456 8704 9 (print)
ISBN 978 1 4456 8705 6 (ebook)

Typesetting by Aura Technology and Software Services, India.
Printed in Great Britain.

Contents

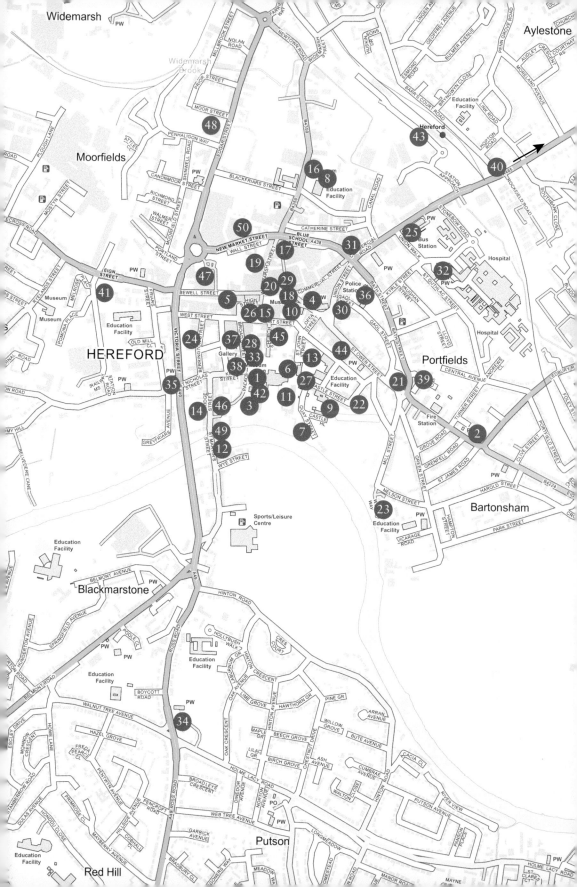

Key

Introduction

Hereford began as the Roman town of Magnis, 3 miles to the west at Kenchester. It lies directly south of Credenhill, a large Iron Age hill fort. The first settlement at Hereford was St Guthlac's monastery. It was built on a terrace on the north bank of the River Wye, adjacent to the only ford with a rock base, just below the Victoria Suspension Bridge. The site of the monastic settlement is now Castle Green.

The creation of the see of Hereford followed, and the first cathedral was built on the terrace to the west of St Guthlac's precinct. This may have been in the present St John's Quad, adjacent to the Lady Chapel, where traces of a large timber building have recently been excavated. A massive stone wall underneath the Cathedral Barn (see No. 6) may well have been part of the precinct boundary of this early building.

It was probably during the late ninth or tenth century that the whole of the city became fully defended, first by a simple rampart and ditch, later with a strong stone face. On the west it came from the riverbank up the eastern side of Victoria Street, then turned east on the line of West Street and East Street, finally curving to the south to include St Guthlac's precinct on its way back to the river. A section is exposed with an access through the car park to the rear of St Owen's Court on the south of St Owen Street.

Hereford's importance was as a city on the border with Wales. It was overrun by the Welsh in 1055 causing considerable damage. As a result the neglected defences were repaired and the ditch was recut. By this time there was probably a royal palace or small castle in the space between the cathedral and St Guthlac's precincts.

Shortly after the Norman Conquest a fine new marketplace (now High Town) was built to the north of the Saxon defences. Construction of the extended defences followed, initially as a rampart and ditch, then fully walled with stone gates. The present Newmarket Street, Blueschool Street and Bath Street are just outside the line of these defences.

The events of the battles for the Crown between Stephen and Matilda (the Anarchy) had a considerable effect on the city. The castle was besieged with engines of war on the cathedral tower, and the whole of St Guthlac's precinct was dug up to provide ramparts, including the mount that still survives at the north-eastern corner of Castle Green. As a result St Guthlac's moved to a new site outside the walled city and the castle was rebuilt and expanded to include the old precinct as the castle bailey.

By the late thirteenth century all hopes of Welsh independence had died and as a result Hereford lost much of is importance. The Civil War in the seventeenth century had some effect on the city, but towards the end of the eighteenth century the defences were considered to be redundant and the gates were all taken down 'to allow the free circulation of air in the town'!

Hereford has since grown well outside its defensive walls, but the central area still reflects its Saxon and Norman layout.

The 50 Buildings

1. Hereford Cathedral

According to tradition the see of Hereford was founded in AD 676, but no trace of the first cathedral has been found. The present Cathedral Church of St Mary and St Ethelbert is mainly of the early twelfth century. It stands in the rather open Close (which was originally the cathedral burial ground) with the Bishop's Palace to the south-west, the college of Vicars' Choral to the east, and other cathedral residential buildings lining the north side.

Aerial view of Hereford Cathedral from the north-west.

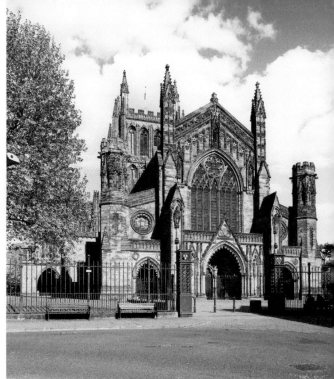

Above left: The nave looking east.

Above right: The cathedral west front.

The main building is of relatively standard design with nave, chancel, transepts and a Lady Chapel at the eastern end. The west front is comparatively new, for the original one, including a massive tower and part of the nave collapsed on Easter Monday in 1786. A large part of the replacement nave was designed by James Wyatt in 1788, while the present west front was built to a design by John Oldrid Scott in 1902–08.

It was in 1140, during the Anarchy (the dispute between Stephen and Matilda for the Crown), that the cathedral effectively became a castle. It was then that the central tower was used as a base for throwing 'missile weapons' against the king's men in the castle. The castle was between the cathedral precinct and St Guthlac's Priory. During the battle, the disturbance to St Guthlac's, which then had the city burial rights, was such that in 1144 it moved to a new site outside the walled town.

Inside the cathedral, the north transept holds two outstanding monuments, which are a main visitor attraction. One is that of Bishop Aquablanca (d. 1268), which is between the transept and the north aisle, while the other, standing more central to the transept, is the tomb chest of St Thomas de Cantilupe (d. 1287). The bright canopy, designed by Robert Kilgour, was placed there after restoration works in 2008.

The most recent artwork in the cathedral is a magnificent sculpture and stained-glass window dedicated to the Special Air Service, which is based in Herefordshire.

2. St Giles Hospital and Chapel, St Owen Street

Situated well outside the medieval city wall, on the corner of St Owen Street and Ledbury Road are two sets of almshouses (or hospitals) – Williams and St Giles. Immediately to the west is the twentieth-century rebuilt St Giles Chapel, which was founded in the twelfth century.

The original chapel site was directly on the road junction, making the crossing very dangerous for pedestrians and motorists. The building, which was built in 1682, was demolished in 1927 and the replacement chapel built to the west reusing the old materials.

But there was an exciting find on the old site. It was examined by Alfred Watkins, a famous local historian and archaeologist, and he uncovered the remains of the twelfth-century chapel. This had a circular nave with an apse and, although it was not possible to preserve the remains, some 13 feet of the roadside garden wall was built on top of the twelfth-century foundations to give a slight impression of the circular building. This still survives and a small plaque commemorating the event is attached. Round churches are typical of the Knights Templar and Hospitallers, so it seems likely that it was administered by the latter body. They were assigned some land by the king in 1158, a date consistent with the physical remains.

It should, perhaps, be noted that there was a second house also dedicated to St Giles in the suburb outside Eign Gate, which existed by 1250.

An odd event occurred in 1321 when Bishop Adam Orleton permitted one Alice de Adforton to be an anchoress in St Giles Church in the suburbs of Hereford.

St Giles Hospital.

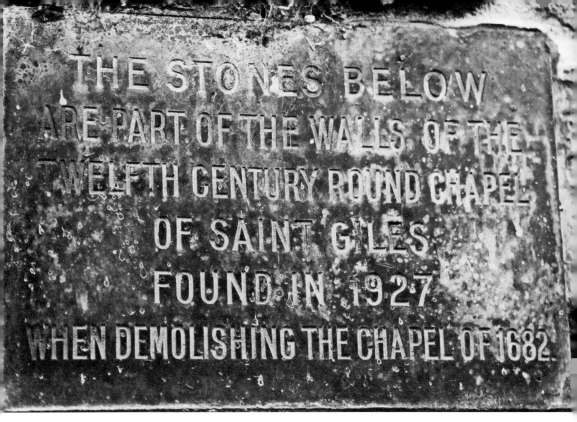

Above: Plaque indicating the site of the round chapel.

Below: The entrance to St Giles Hospital.

The new chapel at St Giles is small with a bell-cote. It contains much of the furniture and fittings, from the original building. Williams' Almshouses still has a plaque dated '1678' but was rebuilt in 1893. Secured to the west wall of St Giles's Hospital is a Romanesque twelfth-century tympanum of Christ blessing with supporting angels. It is much eroded. The present St Giles Hospital was built in 1770 and is single storey with dormers.

3. The Bishop's Palace, Hereford Cathedral

The Bishop's Palace, which can be seen from across the River Wye, stands in large grounds to the south of the cathedral. The grounds and palace are accessed through a gated archway at the southern end of Broad Street. The main part of the building was probably built by William de Vere (bishop 1186–98).

The earliest part of the palace is the surviving wall of the late eleventh-century chapel, which was a structure of the double-chapel type common in Germany and northern France. The initial building took the form of an aisled hall, some 32 metres long by 17 metres wide, with masonry gable ends and aisle walls, but with a timber-framed arcade and a clerestory. It had four bays with a porch in the west wall, and a narrow chamber block of three floors over a basement built at right-angles against the south gable wall. This would have been a fine example of a timber-framed lordly hall with a central fireplace open to the roof. It reflected

The west front of the Bishop's Palace.

Norman roof timbers in the Bishop's Palace.

the most up-to-date styles and was fit for the marcher lord who was also bishop. It is one of the grandest twelfth-century timber buildings to survive in England.

The building has undergone many transformations over the centuries, with large-scale work by Bishop Bisse (1712–21) and by Bishops Huntingford and Musgrave during the first half of the nineteenth century, during which the hall was truncated and turned into a two-storey entrance hall. Within this hall, six of the original posts survive, representing three bays, and the arches connecting these posts can be seen in the attics. One of the arches that was removed during this work is on display in the gatehouse entrance to the palace grounds.

At some stage a much larger chamber block was built to the east of the hall and attached to it by a covered passage. This block was demolished during the nineteenth century. Any remains of this chamber block are now well-buried underneath the lawn to the east of the palace and remain a treat for future archaeologists.

4. St Peter's Church, St Peter's Square

The parish church of St Peter stands on the north side of St Peter's Square. It was founded shortly after the Norman Conquest by Walter de Lacy, who died after a fall from the tower in 1085. In 1101 the church was given by his son, Hugh de Lacy, to the abbey of St Peter at Gloucester. Nothing remains of this early church.

The south face of St Peter's Church.

The late twelfth- or early thirteenth-century chancel is the earliest part of the building. On the south, the tower and south chapel were added in the latter part of the thirteenth century. The nave was rebuilt around 1300 along with the north and south aisles. A restoration in 1793 and further extensive work in the early 1880s removed much of the earlier architecture. However, inside, the royal arms of William III are over the south doorway in the south aisle. The two ranges of quire stalls dating from 1430 to 1450 are noteworthy. They are said to have been brought from St Guthlac's after the Dissolution of the Monasteries. Also from the priory is the large but simple St Guthlac's Cross, which is on display in front of the altar, leaning against the side wall.

St Peter's was the church associated with Revd John Venn (born in 1802 at Clapham where his father was rector). He came to St Peter's in 1833 and, following his father's example, he set about establishing a parish school nearby, on the far side of the road. The foundation stone was laid in 1837 and the school, for both boys and girls, opened on 10 January 1839. This was the beginning of his many contributions to the city and county. Many of the schemes were based on combining industry with charity,

St Guthlac's Cross in
St Peter's Church.

and with this in mind he set up the Hereford Society for Aiding the Industrious. Among his many achievements were the John Venn Mill building, Kyrle Street cottages, and the Working Boys' Home – all in Bath Street. John Venn died in 1890 and is buried in St Peter's graveyard. This is in Commercial Road and is approached through the appropriately named Venn's Arch, now a Grade II listed building.

5. All Saints Church, High Street

The parish church of All Saints stands in High Street facing the northern end of Broad Street, just outside what was once the north gate that led into the Saxon city. The church consists of a nave and chancel with a south aisle and south chapel facing High Street. There is a north aisle and north chapel with the tower at the north-western corner. The upper part of the spire was rebuilt and straightened in 1993. The present building is essentially of late thirteenth- to early fourteenth-century date, but internally there is some evidence of an earlier-thirteenth-century church incorporated in the side walls of the chancel, including parts of a large pier with arches springing in four directions. The roof

Left: The south face of All Saints Church.

Below: The south-west corner of All Saints Church with the south gallery. This area is now used as 'The Café @ All Saints'.

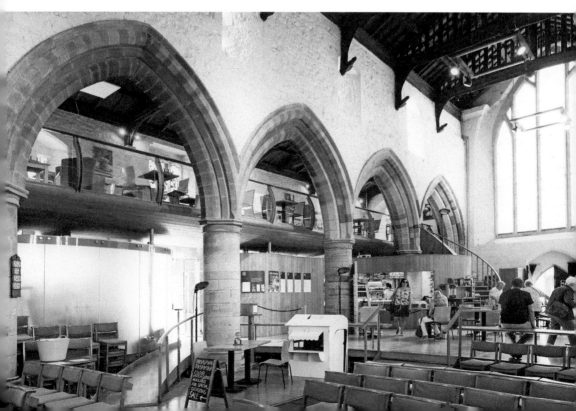

of the south aisle gallery is of king-post construction with carved spandrels, including one of a rather explicit male figure.

The church was restored in 1853 when the north and west galleries were removed, and the organ moved to the south aisle so that the interior 'was converted' from one of the gloomiest 'into one of the most cheerful places of worship'. This was followed by further restoration at the end of the nineteenth century and the beginning of the twentieth, under the auspices of John Oldrid Scott. Restoration under the direction of Rod Robinson Associates between 1992 and 1997 included rebuilding of the upper part of the spire, which had become twisted. Internal work including a new raised floor in the western half of the building, which provided a platform for the innovative use of this area and the rebuilt south gallery as a café, for which it won an award. This latter work also included 'pods' for the vestry, kitchen, servery and an office above the toilets, all without damaging the earlier floor, which remains sealed below the platform. At the same time the opportunity was taken to include the chained library belonging to the church in the cathedral library. The 'Café at All Saints' continues to be popular with townspeople and tourists alike.

6. The Cathedral Barn, Cathedral Close

The barn, now used as a Schools' Centre for the cathedral, stands at the north-eastern corner of the Close. Archaeological excavations have shown that it stood on top of the remains of a massive wall, assumed to be a boundary wall for

The roof of the Cathedral Barn.

The Cathedral Barn with the statue of Sir Edward Elgar.

the Close, in use until the late sixteenth or early seventeenth century. It follows that the building of the barn must be later than that date. However, a detailed survey in 1987 by the City of Hereford Archaeology Unit indicated that it was of thirteenth-century origin with a later phase in the fifteenth century. These conclusions were reinforced in 1996 when samples of the main timbers were taken for dendrochronological dating. The earliest samples provided a felling range of 1253–88, while samples from the later period gave a precise date of 1491.

The tree-ring dates were incompatible with the presence of the stone precinct wall. The only solution was that the barn was a sixteenth-century recycled prefab! All timber-framed buildings are first laid out in a framing yard, where the joints are carefully made and marked with numbers. When all the parts of the frame have been completed, the timbers are taken to the construction site and the building can then be quickly erected. The reverse is, of course, true, and the building can easily be taken down and re-erected on another site. This must have been what happened to the Cathedral Barn, which originally would have been on a different site. Its new use was probably as a grain store for the cathedral bakehouse across the Close.

There were sufficient remains of this earlier building to reconstruct a reasonably accurate picture of what had been a medieval structure, probably aisled and of four bays. Substantial parts of the original building, including aisle posts and arcade plates were reused in the barn. The lower parts of the south wall and the end gables were rebuilt in stone in the seventeenth century. The wattle-and-daub infill was probably replaced with bricks in the eighteenth century.

In the Close, facing the barn, is a statue of the famous composer Sir Edward Elgar (1857–1934), complete with his bicycle.

7. Castle Cliffe on Castle Green

Hereford Castle stood at the eastern end of the city, overlooking the River Wye. The present Castle Green was the bailey of the castle, and before that it was the site of St Guthlac's Priory. The Victoria Suspension Bridge crosses the Wye at its eastern end. Although there are ramparts surrounding the bailey and a small section of the water-filled moat, all the buildings have disappeared, with the exception of Castle Cliffe, which stands close to the riverbank at the south-western corner of the bailey. It is a complex building that has had a variety of uses during its life. The western stone part of the building (now a private house), contains the earliest features including three thirteenth-century doorways and two fourteenth-century windows. The earliest use of the building was as the watergate to the castle. In a survey of the castle in 1652, shortly after the Civil War, it was called 'the Governor's Lodge'.

Castle Cliffe from across the River Wye.

At some time before the beginning of the eighteenth century the building became the City Bridewell or House of Correction. In front of it, on the bank of the Wye, was a wharf. The main building was eventually considered to be unsatisfactory as a gaol and was sold to a Mr H. Hawkins in 1800 for £500. It is now partly a private house and a self-catering holiday property.

The adjoining later building, which faces onto the Green, was built as a cottage to the design of Robert Smirke. It was later expanded with the addition of bathing and reading rooms. It became the meeting room for the Hereford Natural History, Philosophical, Antiquarian and Literary Society (eventually absorbed by the Woolhope Club). Sometime later it was home to the Science and Arts School of the Technical College. It is now called the Pavilion and is used by the Friends of Castle Green for community purposes. The basement, approached by external steps, is used by the Hereford Youth Canoe Club.

8. Blackfriars Monastery, Widemarsh Street

The ruins of the monastery lie well outside the medieval walls and Widemarsh Gate on the eastern side of the main road leading north.

The Dominicans, Black Friars or Friars Preachers arrived in England shortly after AD 1200, having been founded in Spain. They reached Hereford in the mid-thirteenth century and settled on a site at the Portfields outside St Owen's Gate.

The ruins of Blackfriars Monastery.

The Blackfriars Preaching Cross.

After much friction about that site, it was around 1319 that Edward II, Sir John Daniel and the Bishop of Hereford granted them the land that formed the nucleus of the Widemarsh Street site. The priory precinct was walled with a gate onto Widemarsh Street.

Following the Dissolution of the Monasteries, the priory was suppressed on 25 August 1538. There were various owners of the site until 1562 when it passed to Sir Thomas Coningsby of Hampton Court near Leominster. He converted part of the priory to form his town house and took down much of the remainder to build the almshouses known as the Coningsby Hospital (see No. 16). These were built in 1614 on the Widemarsh Street frontage of the site. Coningsby's house was approached through a gatehouse, which is now the southern part of the hospital (No. 108 Widemarsh Street). The house did not survive for long and may well have been damaged during the Civil War, for it was certainly in ruins by 1685.

The surviving ruins (Coningsby's house) comprise the west range of the priory cloister. Part of the east wall, incorporating two three-light window openings, is substantially medieval, but much of the rest, including fireplaces, doorways, windows and the stair tower, is Coningsby's work.

The preaching cross is of fourteenth-century date and is the only surviving example in England of a friars preaching cross. It stood in the cemetery, now laid to lawns with delightful rose gardens.

9. No. 29 Castle Street, the Original Home of the Vicars' Choral

In 1395 the Vicars' Choral were incorporated into a college by Richard II as *Collegium vicariorum in choro ecclesie Herefordensis*, and it is usually assumed that No. 29 Castle Street, the college's first home, dated from that period.

However, a licence from the chapter in 1336 had already granted a habitation in Castle Street to the Vicars' Choral, and a charter of 1375 describes how an old, blind vicar choral, Roger de Clehungre, was assigned property in Hungery Street (now St Owen Street) in exchange for a room called the cysterne chamber in the communal house of the vicars in Castle Street, and a promise that he should receive meals in their common hall for life. This may imply that the Vicars' Choral building was already in place before 1395 and possibly before 1375.

The 10-metre-long and 6.7-metre-wide hall, which lies behind the present Georgian façade, is built of old red sandstone at right angles to the street and has a fine timber roof of nine narrow bays with rather splendid, cusped wind braces. Two tall, narrow windows survive on either side of the building, and the matching doorways (now blocked) to the screens passage remain at the north end of the hall. Little is known about the layout of the rest of the original building. There is a seventeenth-century timber-framed wing and the present frontage is part of a red-brick terrace of early nineteenth-century date.

No. 29 Castle Street exterior.

Above: Roof timbers in No. 29 Castle Street.

Below: The courtyard at No. 29 Castle Street.

As far as the Vicars' Choral were concerned, however, the new building was not an unqualified success. The Vicars' Choral complained that some of their number could not attend the midnight service, because of the distance from the cathedral and the dangers from 'evil-doers'.

The Castle Street building was their home for around a hundred years, which was when plans for a new building to house the Vicars' Choral, to the south-east of the cathedral and east of the Bishop's Palace garden, were approved (No. 11).

10. The Booth Hall, East Street

The earliest record in the Hereford Corporation Archives is of a grant on 28 September 1392 'of the tenement called "Bothealle" to three people by Henry Cachepolle', which indicates that a hall existed at that time and that this meeting room was used for the Merchants Guild. This was an earlier building, for tree-ring dating has shown that the timbers within the present building were cut down somewhere between 1454 and 1492.

It is uncertain when the present Booth Hall actually became an inn, but it must have been before 1686 when Thomas Parry declared that 'Hee was att the Cockpitt at Peter Seabornes house called the Booth Hall seeing a cockfitting'.

In the early part of the nineteenth century the Booth Hall had a notable landlord. This was Thomas Winter Spring (1795–1851). He was a bare-fist fighter

The exterior of the Booth Hall.

Roof timbers in the Booth Hall.

and achieved fame in 1821 as the 'Champion of All England'. After his illustrious career, Tom Spring took over the Booth Hall Inn for several years.

For many years the precise whereabouts of the Booth Hall itself was unknown. It was only rediscovered in 1919 when a chimney stack fell, exposing the magnificent medieval roof timbers. The original building consisted of six bays with alternate tie-beam and hammer-beam trusses, but several bays to the north were lost many years ago. The hammer-beams include figures of angels facing downwards, while cusped wind-braces form arches and quatrefoils in the roof.

For a considerable time the historic hall was not the main part of the inn – this was the nineteenth-century range that extended from the hall towards East Street and included an impressive assembly room that stretched through the present first and second floors. At this time the historic Booth Hall was partitioned into several small rooms with a ceiling concealing the elaborate timber framing. The Booth Hall was almost lost a few years ago when the adjoining Alban House suffered a major fire.

11. Vicars' Choral College, Hereford Cathedral Close

The site chosen in 1472 for the replacement (and present) College for the Vicars' Choral was to the south of the cathedral, where there had previously been houses for two of the canons. One of them formed the basis for the new college hall; the cloister adjoined it to the north.

Above: The Vicars' Choral College from the Cathedral Tower.

Below: The Cloister of the Vicars' Choral College.

The cloister was built of sandstone with an open arcade to the courtyard. The north, east and west ranges of the cloister are similar in length, but the south range is considerably shorter. The college contained twenty-seven units, each with two rooms. In each unit the upper, larger room projected over the cloister, while the lower room was separated from the cloistral walk by a timber-framed wall of close studding. Each room was provided with a fireplace. Eventually the central two-storey lodging on the east side was replaced with a chapel and a library above.

In recognition of the vicars' original complaint, a covered passageway was added between the north-eastern corner of the cloister and the south-east transept of the cathedral, allowing the vicars to reach the cathedral unmolested.

The custos (warden) occupied one of the lodgings in the north range. There was also a kitchen to the south, where a cook concocted the meals that the vicars ate communally in their hall on the south of the cloister.

The reduction in the number of vicar's choral in the post-Reformation period led to several of the lodgings being amalgamated to make larger houses. The hall was extended in 1783 before the Three Choirs Festival.

A disastrous fire in 1828 in the south-west end of the southern range, which had previously been the preserve of the butler and other servants, led to this part of the cloister being rebuilt in brick. To the south of the fire-damaged area was a building used by the canons as a brewery. They obviously had a fine life in the cloister!

12. Old Wye Bridge

The first crossing of the Wye at Hereford was by a ford, and the most likely position was close to St Guthlac's Priory, near the present suspension bridge where there is a rocky base to the river. It is unlikely that there was a satisfactory crossing of the river in the centre of Hereford before a bridge was built as the riverbed there consists of loose gravel.

The date of the first bridge across the Wye at Hereford is uncertain, but there was certainly one there before 1100 when Bishop de Capella provided timber and stone from Haywood Forest for its reconstruction. In 1303 Edward I granted timber for its repair, and in 1383 Richard II provided thirty oaks and forty perches of stone for the same purpose after it had been broken and destroyed by the force of water. These early bridges were probably based on stone piers with a wooden superstructure and would have been built by Royal command.

The present bridge was built *c.* 1490, but a recent survey has indicated that the builders may have made use of some of the earlier piers. The bridge has six arches and five piers and originally had a gatehouse at the southern end.

In 1645, when the Scottish Army attacked Hereford from the south, the third arch from the city was taken down to prevent access. The attack was ferocious and the gate was severely battered, the ruins being completely demolished in 1782.

For centuries the main road along the Welsh border crossed the Wye at the Old Wye Bridge. In 1826 it was widened, just sufficiently to take two lanes of traffic

Above: The Old Wye Bridge with the cathedral in the background.

Below: An eighteenth-century engraving of the Wye Bridge.

– it should be noted that the triangular refuges are on *Ireland's Picturesque Views on the River Wye* (1797) print.

In the southern refuge on the east side are two vertical grooves filled with cement, but they were obviously designed to accommodate some structure. If the conscientious viewer leans over the bridge they will see the next piece of evidence – a pipe leading out from the refuge just below the internal ground level. Have you guessed? The grooves took waist-high slabs of slate to protect the occupant using the urinal, which is shown on the 1886 1:500 Ordnance Survey Map.

13. No. 5, Harley Court, off Cathedral Close

At the north-east corner of the Cathedral Close, close to the statue of Sir Edward Elgar, there is a narrow passage leading eastwards and then north to exit into East Street close to the rear of the Town Hall grounds.

Along this passage, where it turns north, are two semi-detached houses, confusingly numbered 4 and 5 Harley Close. The southernmost (No. 5) was the home of Alfred Watkins from 1919, after his family had grown up, until his death in 1935. Alfred is perhaps best known as a photographer, and the inventor of an early version of the photographic light meter (the bee meter). He also had a great interest in archaeology and was responsible for the excavation of several sites in the city. He had his quirks, however, and will always be remembered for his 1921 theory

The exterior of Nos 4 and 5 Harley Close.

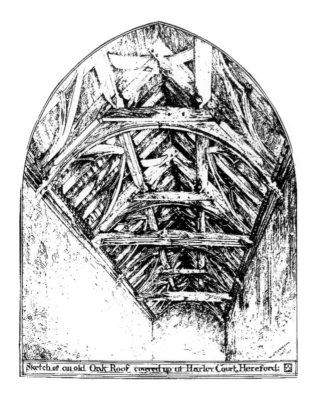

Victorian sketch of the roof of No. 5 Harley Close.

concerning 'ley lines' – the 'old straight tracks' of our historic ancestors. He spent much of the remainder of his life expanding this, pointing out straight tracks around Cambridge and London as well as those in Herefordshire and the Welsh Marches.

When Alfred moved to No. 5 Harley Close, the timber roof of the hall was completely hidden by a false ceiling, although it had been drawn in 1884, before being hidden. The false ceiling has since been removed to expose the finely decorated roof timbers of a fifteenth-century hall that was once probably the home of one of the canons of the cathedral. It was apparent that the hall was much earlier than the building to which it had become attached, which, although timber framed, is some 150 years later in date than the hall. This new building had a huge central chimney stack.

The Elizabethan-style building, along with the earlier hall, is now completely disguised by the whole having been faced with bricks in early Georgian days, when it was divided into two separate houses – Nos 4 and 5 Harley Close.

14. The Black Lion Inn, Bridge Street

The Black Lion Inn is on the west side of Bridge Street not far from the Old Wye Bridge. Although the image of the black lion in many parts of the country refers to one of the heraldic devices of Phillipa, wife of Edward III, there is a chance that the one used in Hereford was associated with Owain Glyndwr, who had a black lion in his arms. This is one of the oldest inns in Hereford, the main part of the building

Above: The Black Lion Inn in Bridge Street.

Below: Part of the Black Lion courtyard in the early twentieth century.

The painted room in the Black Lion.

dating back to the middle or second half of the sixteenth century. It was between the wars that the plaster render was removed from the front elevation, exposing the excellent seventeenth-century timber framing. The grounds were originally long and narrow, stretching back as far as the city wall, which still forms its western boundary. Early in the twentieth century the narrow property to the south was added to the Black Lion and, following demolition, provided a good vehicular access to the courtyard and the several buildings at the rear of the inn itself.

A room on the first floor of the inn was used as a club room for many years. It has a plaster ceiling enriched with a central oval and a plaster overmantel with four blank arches. Also in the room are the remains of series of wall paintings representing people breaking the Ten Commandments, which were discovered in 1932. The first three were destroyed many years ago, and the series now begins with the Fourth Commandment – 'remember that thou keep holy the Sabbath day'. Appropriately it shows a man gathering sticks. It is not suggested that these paintings represent the landlord and his customers, but it is interesting to note that, following the restoration of the monarchy in 1660, various members of the cathedral's Vicars' Choral began to join in the social life of the city and had 'frequent carousels at the Black Lion Club Room'! It is suggested that the murals may have been painted by John Gildon, who carved several tombs in the area in the late sixteenth century.

15. The Grapes Tavern, Church Street

The Grapes Tavern is now a well-cared-for and attractive pub, situated at the corner of East Street and the narrow pedestrian part of Church Street, which leads through from East Street to High Town. It is surrounded by the vast Marks & Spencer store to the north and west.

Right: The Grapes Tavern with the narrow passage leading to High Town on the right.

Below: An early photograph of the Reading Room at The Grapes.

The Grapes overlies the Saxon defences of Hereford. It was probably originally built at some time during the seventeenth century, but has been much restored. In the early nineteenth century it was known as the Royal Oak and Grapes – a much more dignified title. When, in 1839, it was put up for auction, it was described as 'the extensive and old established inn ... fronting Church Street, the greatest thoroughfare in the city leading to the cathedral. The House consists of a roomy and well appointed Bar, three large Parlours and Taproom, cooking Kitchen etc.' It was around this time, or a little later, that the Grapes had an official reader, appointed yearly, of the *London Letter*, which was delivered weekly by stagecoach. Until recently the reading room survived. The chairs, set against the walls, were occupied by men who 'were duly and solemnly elected to them', and it was here that substantial tradesmen met every evening to drink, smoke and gossip. The news of the fall of Sebastopol (in 1854) and that of the Indian Mutiny (in 1857) were both read out in this room. Sadly the newsroom has lost much of its character by being opened through to the rear and the armed seating has been removed.

The inn was closed in 1988 due to serious structural failings. A survey at that time demonstrated that the Grapes consisted of three separate buildings, two seventeenth century in date and one of the late eighteenth century. The problem was that the whole front of the building was about to fall into East Street and had to be completely rebuilt. The opportunity was taken to roof over the small courtyard and to move the main entrance from East Street onto the much safer pedestrianised Church Street.

16. Coningsby Hospital, Widemarsh Street

Well outside the medieval walled city, Coningsby Hospital was founded by Sir Thomas Coningsby on part of the site that had been occupied by the Dominican Black Friars Priory until the Dissolution of the Monasteries. Coningsby converted part of the priory to become his town house, and then took down much of the remaining buildings to form the hospital, which was built in 1614, on the Widemarsh Street frontage (No. 8).

The hospital was built around a courtyard, with a hall and chapel on the north side and twelve one-up-one-down tenements in the other sides. The number was increased to thirteen when the gatehouse, on the south of the almshouses, that had originally led to Coningsby's house, was converted following the Civil War.

The buildings were restored by John Gray in 1854 to include a nineteenth-century pump in the courtyard to provide water for the inmates. More recently, the tenements have been redesigned to include a kitchen and bathroom in each, along with a water supply. Originally the inmates, who were war veterans, had to wear a red uniform – there are several examples in the museum. These may be linked to Nell Gwynne, who suggested the Chelsea Hospital in London to Charles II. She was born in Hereford.

Above: Coningsby Hospital in Widemarsh Street.

Right: Part of the courtyard at Coningsby Hospital in the early twentieth century.

The chapel has many features of interest, including a family pew with the initials of Sir Thomas and his wife Philippa, dated 1597, and the stained-glass east window of 1869, which was taken from the former parish church of St Denis at Harewood.

The hall is now a two-storey museum with the chapel to the east, and is regularly open to the public. On the ground floor there is a glass plate in the floor, where a skeleton can be seen. Was he once a warrior and finally a resident in the hospital? The first floor, which overlooks the chapel, was probably originally used as the infirmary.

17. The Cosy Club (until recently the Farmers' Club), No. 42 Widemarsh Street

The Cosy Club is a large historic building on the east side of Widemarsh Street, immediately inside the city wall, part of which forms the building's northern wall. Until 1798, when it was demolished, the Widemarsh Gate, leading into the medieval city from the north, adjoined the northern half. Until recently the building had, for many years, been the Farmers' Club.

In the late sixteenth century Thomas Church, a dyer, and his wife were tenants of the building. He had recently 'erected and built one newe roome' attached to the building. The new room was presumably his dye house, and must have been built directly against the city wall, for some years later he asked permission to make 'one litle doore through the Towne wall to thend the said orator may the better washe his coloured clothes', presumably in the city ditch. The 'doore' still remains and has his initials and the date 1626 (just visible) carved on the lintel. The main building has been dated to 1617.

There was further modernisation during the early part of the eighteenth century, using ashlar on the ground floor of the southern part of the Widemarsh Street elevation and including new windows at ground- and first-floor level to create the impression of a four-bay early Georgian house. The demolition of the gatehouse meant that the northern part of the elevation had to be rebuilt, which accounts for the difference in the masonry. The site of the original front door in Widemarsh Street has some fine Jacobean carving on the brackets.

At the beginning of the nineteenth century the building became a girls' school, run by Miss Croucher. She employed the famous artist David Cox as a drawing master at a salary of £100 per annum. In the latter half on the nineteenth century it changed to become a private boys' school run by Revd W. Bowell. Charles Watkins sent his son Alfred there, and many years later Alfred told his son 'that it was a shocking bad school, where the teaching was perfectly dreadful, and I learnt absolutely nothing'. The change to the Farmers' Club must have been welcome!

The Cosy Club was for many years known as the Farmers' Club.

Above: Carving above the original front door.

Right: The 'little doore' in the city wall.

18. The Old House, High Town

The date on the shield held by angels underneath the central gable is 1621. The design and construction may well have been an early work of John Abel of Sarnesfield, who, after the Civil War, became the king's carpenter in 1645.

The house was originally part of The Butchery and is shown as such on Taylor's 1757 map of the city. The arms of the Butchers' Guild of London are carved on a shield above the door in the south porch, but there is no known connection.

The Wathen painting of 1798 and the Cox one of 1815 both show buildings on both sides of the Old House; however by the time Cox completed his painting the building on the right, then being used as an earthenware shop, had been demolished. All the buildings in The Butchery (or Butchers' Row) were pulled down by 1837 as they were described as 'a great annoyance, and that it would add much to the ornament and convenience of the city to take the said buildings down'. Fortunately the Old House survived!

The first occupant of the Old House was probably John Jones, a butcher, and it continued to be a butcher's shop and residence for many years. By the middle of the nineteenth century it had become a saddler, then later in that century a hardware shop. Its final use was as a branch of the Worcester City and County Banking Co., which eventually became Lloyds Bank. In 1928, the bank erected a

The Old House in High Town.

Above: The entrance porch to the Old House.

Below: An interior view of the Old House.

new building on the north side of High Town and gave the Old House to the city of Hereford for use as a museum.

Today the building has been arranged to show the domestic arrangements of an early seventeenth-century house from the kitchen, through the living rooms and upstairs to the bedrooms.

19. The Mansion House, Widemarsh Street

The Mansion House stands on the western side of Widemarsh Street, approximately halfway between High Town and Newmarket Street.

It was built in 1697 for Dr William Brewster of Burton Court and was one of the earliest brick-faced houses in Hereford. It was probably part of a substantial rebuild of this part of Widemarsh Street. It is a two-and-a-half storey, five-bay structure with finely cut red bricks laid to a Flemish bond. At that time the plot

The Mansion House in Widemarsh Street.

behind his house contained an inn and a bowling green, as well as the dwelling house garden.

The building originally had a central hall, with a main door to Widemarsh Street and, at the rear, next to the central staircase, a door to the garden. After varied ownership, including Hereford City Council (who hoped to use it for their offices) by 1796 'the premises were much fallen into decay'.

After several changes of ownership, in the early twentieth century it passed to George Wright, who gutted the ground floor by making an open passageway to the rear to accommodate a jam factory. In the process the central staircase, which was probably of dog-leg design, was removed.

The passageway now leads through a car park to the Tesco supermarket. Some years ago this passageway was named Alfred Watkins's Way. This upset his daughter, who thought that her father's memory deserved more than a miserable passageway, and the name was rapidly changed to Mansion House Way. The rooms on each side of the passageway are now occupied by modern full-depth shops, and the jam factory has totally disappeared.

20. The Merchant's House, Nos 6–8 Widemarsh Street

This is one of the most fascinating historic houses in Hereford, for it was only rediscovered some twenty years ago. Although in the centre of the city and only a few yards from High Town, its access is by a narrow passage leading from the eastern side of Widemarsh Street into a small courtyard, and it backs onto Nos 3–5 High Town (all now shops).

All the features, including the staircase, with its closed string, and the cross window, indicate a construction date during the final stages of the seventeenth century. The hand-made bricks are of a dusky colour – probably originally fired with Forest of Dean coal brought up the River Wye.

Only the western part of the building survives, the eastern portion having been demolished in 1962. At that time the ground floor was the only part of the building in use, the upper floors having been abandoned since the beginning of the twentieth century. The surviving portion contains a very good original staircase and a moulded plaster ceiling on the first floor, as well as other historic fittings.

There is a cellar underneath the main building which is linked by a vaulted brick passage to the cellars underneath No. 3 High Town and is also connected to a large vaulted brick cellar underneath the courtyard. During the Second World War these cellars, including the ones further up Widemarsh Street and those underneath the Buttermarket, were all connected together to provide a large air-raid shelter.

This forgotten building is now Grade II listed and has Planning Permission and Listed Building Consent to be converted to 1,700 square feet of accommodation over five floors.

The Merchant's House in Widemarsh Street is hidden away.

The fine internal staircase in the Merchant's House.

21. The Barrels, St Owen Street

Many of the roads that led into the medieval city had an inn just outside the gate. St Owen Street was no exception, as a late eighteenth-century watercolour shows. It depicts the outside of St Owen's Gate with an inn sign in a prominent position on the right-hand side, which appears to have a lamb on it. Historically this inn was known as the Lamb and Flag. It later became simply the Lamb (as carved on the frontage elevation above the doorway), and more recently the Barrels.

St Owen's Gate was the main access to the city from the south-east, and although the gate was demolished in the 1780s, the city wall still approaches the street from both the north and south. On the north it forms the boundary between the Barrels and a restaurant called The Taste of Raj. The Barrels is built partly on top of what was the city ditch on the outside of the city wall. This can be best appreciated in the excellent outdoor area at the rear of the inn, where the buttressed city wall forms its western boundary.

Above: The Barrels Inn in St Owen Street.

Below: The city wall in the Barrels Inn garden.

The original door leading into the courtyard is now a window.

Prior to 1967 the narrow road (now called Harrison Street) that runs along the out-of-town side of the Barrels was the southern end of Bath Street – the main road leading towards Ledbury. The delivery entry to the Barrels was then directly from this narrow street. It has since been converted to a large window, but older regulars remember it as having a large green door. There was no other entry to the inn courtyard. At that time the inn had just two rooms – the bar and the snug. The back door was the archway that now adjoins the bar. As part of the Inner Relief Road, a long, curving extension was made to Bath Street, cutting across what had been St Owen's burial ground. The earlier line of Bath Street was then cut off and renamed Harrison Street.

22. Castle House Hotel, Castle Street

The original building almost certainly dates from the earlier part of the eighteenth century, being shown on Taylor's 1757 plan of Hereford as sealing the eastern end of Castle Street and overlooking Castle Pool, the only surviving part of the wet moat that surrounded Hereford Castle. It was originally built as two houses with adjoining front doors and was still shown as such on the 1886 large scale Ordnance Survey plan of the city.

Castle Pool Hotel, Hereford.

Castle House from across the castle moat in 1922.

The front building is three stories high with cellars. Originally each half contained a narrow hall leading to stairs with a morning room to the front and a dining room to the rear, each with a corner fireplace. The service blocks were to the rear again. The front room on the first floor of each house was the drawing room; the rear room on this floor and the two on the second floor made up the three bedrooms.

Early in the 1890s, Frederick Boulton, the owner of both houses, carried out some alterations to the rear service wings and then combined both houses to make a single residence. This involved creating a new central hall by removing much of the spine wall that separated the two houses to provide the wide stairway that graces the present hall. The original two doors were replaced by the present central doorway.

After some years as a private house, by 1922 the building was described as a boarding house, but had become a private hotel by 1926. During the Second World War it was used as a hostel for female workers at the Rotherwas Munitions Factory. As the Castle Pool Hotel, it continued to flourish after the war and obtained a residential licence in July 1967, allowing it to have a public bar. It continues to be a popular hotel in the city and is well used by the citizens of Hereford as well as visitors to the city. It has a fine terraced garden leading down to Castle Pool.

Castle House from Castle Street.

23. General Hospital (former), Nelson Street

The former General Hospital stands on the east bank of the River Wye, a short distance from the Castle Green area. It was originally approached by Mill Street until Nelson Street was cut through to the north-east of the hospital in 1878.

The original General Infirmary, which was opened to patients in Eign Street in 1776, was replaced by the purpose-built General Hospital. It had been the result of serious fundraising by Reverend Dr Thomas Talbot, who was rector of St Luke's Church at Ullingswick for some fifty years. He was a compassionate man who was increasingly concerned for the need of an infirmary. By March 1775, following two appeals, he had raised £3,000 and a committee was set up to organise the project. Six months later Edward Harley donated the land in Hereford near the river, and when the fund reached £4,000 building work started. The foundation stone was laid in 1781 and the infirmary, later the General Hospital, was opened in 1783. Thomas Talbot is still remembered by the people of Ullingswick, who hold a service of evensong every year on the Sunday nearest 18 February – the date of his death in 1789.

The infirmary was built to the design of William Parker. It is of brick, two-and-a-half storeys high and nine bays wide. The central five bays are set forward

The old General Hospital.

with a pediment. Various additions were made, including an extension by F. R. Kempson as the Victoria Wing for children. The Nurses' Home on the south end was added in 1922.

At the end of the twentieth century it was decided that all hospital facilities in Hereford should be centralised on the County Hospital site, and in 2002 the *Hereford Times* reported that the General Hospital site had been sold to Laing Homes for a sum in excess of £3 million. Later additions to the hospital were demolished, but the Grade II buildings were kept and have been converted into flats and apartments.

New buildings at the rear extended to Nelson Street. Archaeologists working on the site before building work commenced excavated the remains of a much earlier building, probably dating from the early years after the Conquest.

24. Gala Bingo Hall, No. 44 Berrington Street

In a side street close to the city centre, this building has had a multitude of uses and is rich in history. It was erected in 1787, one of sixty-four chapels funded by Selina Hastings, Countess of Huntington, a leading light in the Methodist Evangelical Movement. The strict rules 'against a vain conformity of the world in card playing, dancing, frequenting playhouses and places of carnal amusement' were too difficult and in 1885 the building was sold and became the Beethoven Hall – a piano and organ showroom for Messrs Heins. This establishment moved to other premises in 1913 and the building was then converted to a cinema called simply the Picture House. By 1919 there was a further change, when it became the Palladium Theatre, seating some 470 customers.

There were extensive alterations in 1928 when the building was extended by some 18 feet to enlarge the stage, and a canopy was erected along the front. The renovated theatre then had seating for some 600 people. By 1942, with the war at its height, it reverted to showing films. After the war it was reopened by a repertory company – the County Theatre. One of the first plays included Arthur Lowe (Captain Mainwaring of *Dad's Army*), one among many visiting actors to become TV greats.

However, by 1953 it had closed due to lack of support, and then reopened as a 3D, widescreen, cinemascope establishment, with some live shows. A change occurred again in 1957 when it became the County Ballroom and roller-skating

The Beethoven Room at No. 44 Berrington Street around 1900.

The Gala Bingo Hall, Berrington Street.

rink. A little later it was a restaurant and cabaret, then, in the mid-1960s it became the Regal Cinema. After a relatively short time the building had a final change and became the Regal (now Gala) Bingo Hall, a use that has continued for some fifty years. The Countess of Huntington could not possibly have imagined such a use for her Methodist chapel.

25. Governor's House, Union Walk

The building, standing on the edge of the Hereford bus station, containing a shop and three flats, is not one to grab the immediate interest of passers-by, but it has a fascinating history. It is the last surviving part of the county gaol, built to the design of John Nash in 1797 on similar lines to Newgate Gaol in London. The main buildings were laid out on a cruciform shape, the whole being surrounded by a high brick wall. The only entry was from Bye Street Without (now Commercial Road).

The original gaol was quite small, but extensions and alterations made in the first half of the nineteenth century, filled the whole site of the bus station and through to Commercial Road.

By the latter part of the nineteenth century it would have been unacceptable for the prison governor and his family to be accommodated within the confines of the

Above: A view of the County Gaol just before its demolition in 1930.

Below: The Governor's House in Union Walk.

gaol itself. He would have expected to have a house provided that was adjacent to the gaol, but not part of it. The problem was resolved by converting part of the prison to provide him with a reasonably large and separate dwelling with a coach house, stables and gardens. At a later date one bay of the prison was taken down to ensure that the governor's house was totally separate from the prison. This is the building that survives to the present day.

The prison was finally closed in 1929 and demolition of all the prison buildings took place in the following year, leaving the governor's house as the sole reminder of this historic use.

But the gaol was not the earliest use of this large site. From 1144 to the Dissolution of the Monasteries this was part of the site of St Guthlac's Priory, which had moved there from Castle Green after the battles between cousins Stephen and Matilda over the monarchy.

26. Barclays Bank, Broad Street

Barclays bank is on the east side of Broad Street at its northern end. The present building replaced an important city inn – The Swan and Falcon, which had its frontage much further forward, for this was originally the site of the north gate into the Saxon city. The inn was demolished in 1790 to make way for a town house for Charles Howard, 11th Duke of Norfolk, who had been elected as chief steward of the city. However, it was still effectively the Swan and Falcon. In 1795 it became the City Arms, an establishment that continued to operate into the latter part of

Barclays Bank in Broad Street.

the twentieth century; although, in the 1860s the northern wing was demolished to make way for premises for the Gloucestershire Banking Company, later a shop.

Although the inn was successful, having an extension built along East Street in 1798, a long-term problem had begun to manifest itself by the 1960s. The foundations of the building had been laid on the mud of the long-abandoned Saxon city ditch and, although extensive restoration work had been carried out in 1939, the building had started to move. The inn was eventually closed in 1973. Planning permission was then granted for the conversion to a branch of Barclays bank – conditional on the retention of the Georgian façade. The front and side walls were then supported with scaffolding and the internal floors and walls were all removed. In effect, a new building was constructed within the shell of the old City Arms.

Surprisingly not all has been lost for, in the rear part of the bank, part of a timber-framed fifteenth-century building (the old back bar of the City Arms) has survived two demolitions. Also, look closely at the ground-floor windows on either side of the main front doorway to the bank in Broad Street. Although the windows are square, the windowsills still retain the slope caused by the partial collapse of the building into the Saxon ditch.

27. The Old Deanery, Cathedral Close

The Old Deanery stands in its own grounds on the eastern side of the Cathedral Close. It is now part of the Hereford Cathedral School, which occupies several other buildings in the area including some in Castle Street and East Street.

The Old Deanery in the Cathedral Close.

The Courtyard of the Old Deanery.

There was probably a school associated with the cathedral from the foundation of the see in the late seventh century, but the earliest documentary record of the school dates from 1384 when Bishop John Gilbert appointed Richard de Cornwaille as schoolmaster and authorised him 'to rule over the school with birch and rod'. It is presumed that present-day students have a much gentler treatment!

During the following centuries the school attracted several generous benefactors. It was rebuilt during the reign of Edward VI and received grants from Elizabeth I. Sometime before 1762 the school building was again rebuilt after it had fallen into disrepair. In 1875 new classrooms were built in School Yard. The school remained relatively small until the period between the two world wars. It attained grant-aided status in 1945 and by 1970 had expanded to 370 boys (still no girls), most of whom were day pupils. The school became co-educational in 1973 and had boarders until relatively recently. The school is an independent, co-educational day school with some 786 students in 2016.

The Old Deanery is essentially a nineteenth-century building, but with earlier origins. It is built of dressed sandstone on an E-shaped plan, with gable wings. It is listed Grade II. It was taken over by the Cathedral School when the dean moved to smaller and more convenient quarters in the Vicars' Choral College.

28. No. 12 Broad Street

In the early nineteenth century this handsome building was the Mitre Hotel – one of the main coaching inns in Hereford. The name was changed from the Golden Lion to the Mitre around the 1780s. The 'mitre' is the tall cap, deeply cleft at the top, worn by bishops as a symbol of their office and has been a common name for inns in cathedral cities since the fifteenth century. This was appropriate in Hereford, for the building was once owned by St Ethelbert's Hospital, one of the charities connected with the cathedral.

The present building was built about 1805 at a cost of approximately £670. During the earlier part of the nineteenth century there was a hanging balcony across the southern part of the façade, including the drivers' entrance. It was eventually replaced by the present balcony, used regularly as a platform for Tory parliamentary candidates to address their supporters. One of the more recent uses was in 1951, when the then foreign secretary, Anthony Eden, addressed a Broad Street crowd some 1,000 strong.

No. 12 Broad Street, once the Mitre Hotel.

The public entry into the main part of the hotel was through revolving doors into the lounge and saloon bar, but through the driving way and across the yard was the Mitre Vaults, containing public and private bars. At the beginning of the First World War the hotel had thirteen double- and five single-letting bedrooms, but apparently only two bathrooms.

In 1921, the thriller writer Edgar Wallace stayed at the Mitre during the famous nine-day trial of the Hay solicitor Herbert Rouse Armstrong for the murder of his wife. Armstrong, who many people were certain was innocent, was found guilty and hanged at Gloucester Gaol. In a later thriller Wallace referred to the Mitre as having a good cellar of port!

The Mitre finally closed to customers on 28 September 1955 to become the District Bank, later National Westminster. It is now the offices of a firm of solicitors.

29. Buttermarket, High Town

The Buttermarket has an impressive entry on the north side of High Town, and also has entrances from Widemarsh Street and Maylord Street. It was completed in 1816 and replaced the many street markets that had previously been a feature of the city.

The site was previously occupied by the Redstreak Inn – doubtless named after the famous cider apple developed by Viscount Scudamore at his estate at Holme Lacy during and after the Civil War. It had a narrow frontage to High Town, now occupied by the Buttermarket entrance, which provided a driving way to the inn. In the latter part of the eighteenth century the inn was the starting point for coaches from Hereford to London. Although called Preuen's Flying Machine, it took thirty-six hours to complete the journey.

The New Inn in Widemarsh Street had grounds that adjoined the Redstreak and in 1809 the Hereford Council bought both properties in order to build a Council Chamber and poultry and butter market. When built, the Buttermarket was open to the skies, not being covered in for some forty years.

Originally the rear part of the Buttermarket was used as a slaughterhouse. It was in 1860 that the iron and glass roof was constructed. It was also at this time that the present front was built to the design of John Clayton, with the square clock tower and the statues of Bacchus and Ceres by William Boulton of Lambeth.

After a fire in 1922, the interior was reconstructed. The only major change after this was the rather controversial suspended ceiling installed in 2001. Recently proposals have been made to remove it and create a series of stalls on a gallery at first-floor level.

Until relatively recently, there was a sign in the north-west corner of the Buttermarket reading 'Air Raid Shelter'. This was a relic of the Second World War when the market cellar was joined to those of properties in Widemarsh Street through to High Town, creating this large shelter.

A sketch of the proposed Buttermarket by the architect John Clayton.

MARKET HALL

The Buttermarket in High Town.

30. The Shire Hall, St Peter's Square

St Peter's Square, at the eastern end of High Town, includes St Peter's Church on the north and the Shire Hall on the east. The square contains the war memorial, which stands in the centre, and, perhaps rather unfortunately, a series of bus stops. The Shire Hall was built between 1815 and 1817 to the design of Robert Smirke. Facing the square, the sandstone portico is Greek Doric of six columns with plain flanking bays. The Shire Hall is essentially a T-plan with a wide entrance passage flanked by two courtrooms. It leads, up a flight of steps, to the five-bay rear hall with round-arched windows and a stage.

The Shire Hall replaced the county gaol, which was in use throughout the eighteenth century, if not earlier. The gaol was set well back from the road, as is the Shire Hall. However, there are intriguing mentions of vaults in front of the Shire Hall, and some years ago, when a trench was being dug underneath the pavement in front of the forecourt, the workmen broke through into a vaulted chamber underneath the forecourt. Apart from noting the footings for

THE WAR MEMORIAL & SHIRE HALL, HEREFORD.

Above: The Shire Hall and
the war memorial in St Peter's
Square.

Right: The memorial to
Sir George Cornwall Lewis at the
Shire Hall.

SIR
GEORGE CORNEWALL LEWIS.

the memorial statue to Sir George Cornwall Lewis (MP for Hereford, who died in 1864), which apparently cut through the vaulting, the chamber still survives underneath what is now a car park.

Hangings, even for minor crimes, were relatively common and took place in the square in front of the gaol. However, most death sentences for minor offences were commuted. A late one involved the execution of William Jones and Susannah Rugg on 1 August 1790. The pair had conspired together to poison Jones's wife by the use of arsenic. After the execution the body of Jones was taken and hung in chains at Longtown Green, near to his former residence.

The Shire Hall forecourt is flanked by two buildings: on the south a three-bay house for the custodian and, on the north the former police station, built in 1898 to the design of H. T. Wakelam.

31. Play Nightclub, Nos 51–55 Blueschool Street

This building was a Bluecoat School for many years, hence the name of the street. The earliest Blue Coat School was Christ's Hospital in London, founded in 1563. The movement expanded around the country and the Blue Coat School in Hereford was opened in 1710. The site of the Hereford school was formerly a workhouse that was the basis of the school. It does not appear that any building works took place at that time.

It was in 1827 that the street frontage buildings were erected with houses for the master and mistress on each side of the main building. These are the street frontage buildings as seen today.

The Play nightclub in Blueschool Street.

andwork Class. Blue Coat School. Hereford.

A classroom in the Bluecoat School in the early twentieth century.

An entry in the 1891 Kelly's Directory indicates that the school was enlarged in 1889 to accommodate 250 boys and 220 girls. In 1910 an extensive range of buildings was erected to the rear of the earlier school to the design of local architect W. W. Robinson.

Education up to the age of fourteen had become compulsory and in 1910 the school was recognised by the Board of Education as providing accommodation for not more than 200 boys and 180 girls.

In 1921 the Bluecoat School became just a girls' school. The 1944 Education Act provided more changes; the Bluecoat School then being recognised as a secondary school. After the Second World War the school had to take a sudden influx of children, and in 1949 three HORSA Huts (Hutting Operation for Raising of the School-raising Age) were erected on land immediately to the east of the school playground.

By September 1958 there were some 850 girls on the register and the old premises of the High School for Girls in Coningsby Street were then put at the disposal of the Bluecoat School.

On 23 June 1960 there were celebrations to mark the 250th anniversary of the foundation of the Bluecoat School in Hereford. They were held at the Coningsby Street School in the presence of Her Majesty Queen Elizabeth the Queen Mother. Finally the Bluecoat School merged with Bishop's School at Hampton Dene, leading to the new Bishop of Hereford's Bluecoat School, which opened in 1973. Eventually the redundant school buildings in Blueschool Street became the Play nightclub.

32. Former Union Workhouse, County Hospital

The Poor Law Act of 1601 set up a system of relief for the poor by placing the responsibility on the parishes, which lasted through the following two centuries. A new Poor Law Act in 1834 enabled parishes to join together to form unions and share one central workhouse. This is what happened in Herefordshire, the union serving forty-nine parishes.

The Hereford Union Workhouse was opened in 1838, having been built to the design of John Plownan Jr. The building complex stands in the south of the present hospital grounds, facing onto Union Walk.

When built, the workhouse had room for up to 300 inmates and was ruled by a master and matron appointed by the governors. Staff included schoolteachers and a chaplain. Any male inmate had to bring his family with him, but he and his wife were separated, along with all children over seven years of age. Other inmates included unmarried mothers, illegitimate children and widows with children. All, apart from the youngest and the infirm, were made to work hard. Life was intended to be harsh, with menial jobs such as breaking stones, crushing bones for use as fertilisers and picking oakum. The workhouse was extended in 1862 with cross-plan courtyards to the rear. A chapel, which still survives, was added at the western end in 1880.

The residents had a shock at 5.30 a.m. on 17 December 1896, when the famous 'Hereford Earthquake' sent two of the workhouse chimneys crashing through the roof.

The Union Workhouse, which is now part of the County Hospital.

The Union Workhouse Chapel.

One famous resident was Gilbert Harding. His parents were employed as master and matron of the workhouse when he was born in 1907. He was well known as a journalist, television personality and actor. He was a regular on BBC Radio's *Twenty Questions* and was voted Personality of the Year in the National Radio Awards of 1953–54. Harding regularly appeared on the BBC television panel game *What's My Line* as a panellist, having been the presenter of the very first episode in 1951. He died in 1960. The workhouse is now used for hospital purposes.

33. St Francis Xavier Church, Broad Street

St Francis Xavier is a Roman Catholic parish church in the Hereford deanery of the archdiocese of Cardiff, and is administered by Belmont Abbey. It stands on the east side of Broad Street, a short distance north of the Cathedral Close.

Francis Xavier was born in the Kingdom of Navarre (present-day Spain) in 1506. He was a cofounder of the Society of Jesus, and, throughout most of his life he was a Christian missionary, notably in India. He was known as the 'Apostle of the Indies' and the 'Apostle of Japan'. He died in 1552 on his way to China. He was beatified by Pope Paul V in 1619 and canonised by Pope Gregory XV in 1622.

The Catholic church of St Francis Xavier in Broad Street.

The interior of St Francis Xavier Church.

The Hereford neoclassical church was designed by Charles Day of Worcester and opened on 7 August 1839. It cost over £16,000 and is now a Grade II* listed building. It was built on the site of a chapel used by the Society of Jesus during the Reformation – hence the dedication.

The front elevation includes two fluted Doric columns on either side of the entrance, and there is a dome to the rear. The ornate interior includes a decorated plaster ceiling. The altar is flanked by two Ionic columns.

The church contains a Herefordshire relic: the hand of St John Kemble, a Catholic martyr, who was convicted of the treasonable crime of being a Catholic priest and was hung, drawn and quartered on Widemarsh Common in 1679, at the age of eighty. Before he was led out to his execution Father Kemble insisted on saying his prayers and finishing his drink, and the assembled party joined the elderly priest in a final smoke and a cup of sack. The Herefordshire sayings, a Kemble pipe and Kemble cup, refer to a parting pipe or cup. He was beatified in 1929 by Pope Pius XI and canonized by Pope Paul VI in 1970. Apart from his hand, the rest of his body is buried in the Church of England churchyard of St Mary the Virgin at Welsh Newton in Herefordshire.

34. St Martin's Church, Ross Road

The original St Martin's Church was destroyed in 1645 during the siege of the city by the Scottish army in the Civil War. It was situated close to the south bank of the River Wye near the bridge, an area that is now a car park. It probably suffered from both the assailants and the besieged because of its position near the bridge, where there was a gatehouse. Little is known of the early church apart from the fact that it was founded in the thirteenth century and had a steeple and three bells; the altar was dedicated in April 1325. It was a chapel of All Saints' Church.

The new church was built in 1840–45 at a cost of some £5,000 to a design by Robert W. Jearrad, and is well to the south of the original site. Queen Victoria gave £1,000 towards the building fund. It consisted of a nave, two transepts and a chancel. The chancel was extended by Nicholson in 1894–85, including the fine east window. The nave roof is framed and panelled in oak with moulded cross ribs. The building has a thin, west tower with a ribbed spire. The spire was damaged in a strong wind in 1895 and suffered further damage the following year when there was an earthquake. The font of the church is the only relic of the past. It is cut out of solid stone and probably dates from the fourteenth century.

For several years part of the graveyard was the cemetery for the 22nd Special Services Regiment, when they were based close by. This was before their move to Credenhill.

St Martin's Church is south of the River Wye in Ross Road.

The SAS memorial plaque.

35. St Nicholas Church, Friars Street

Before the Norman Conquest there could only have been one church, apart from the cathedral, inside the Saxon city. This was St Nicholas's Church, but there is some uncertainty as its foundation date is unknown. The original St Nicholas's Church was placed in the middle of the road at the intersection of King Street and Bridge Street – really inconvenient as traffic could hardly get past it! It consisted of a nave, a side aisle towards the north, a chancel, and a tower with six bells. Before the dissolution, there were two chantries in honour of the Virgin Mary. The church was heavily restored or rebuilt in 1718 with donations from James, Duke of Chandos, the mayor and council, and others.

The old church was demolished in the mid-nineteenth century, the replacement being placed further to the west and outside the medieval defences on the corner of Friars Street. A grant of £100 from the Church Commissioners was given only on the understanding that the area on which the previous church stood shall be entirely open to the public. In the event of there being any enclosure whatsoever, the £100 would not be advanced. The replacement was the result of a competition with twenty-seven entrants, before the commissioners' church was chosen. This new church was built in 1841–42, to the design of Thomas Duckham. It was built as a preaching hall with box seats and benches, a central pulpit, and was

St Nicholas Church was opened in 1842.

designed to accommodate 570 people. There was a major reordering in 1910 when the chancel was enlarged. In 1939 the space underneath the church floor was 'converted' for use as an air-raid shelter. During these excavations a Norman arch stone was discovered in the basement wall. After the war the organ blower was situated in this underfloor area.

36. The Old City Gaol and Magistrates' Building, Gaol Street

The earliest city gaol was in the southern part of the building associated with Bye Street Gate, the north-eastern entry to the medieval walled city. All the buildings, which were in front of the present Kerry Arms, have since been demolished.

The Gaol Street Gaol was completed by 1844 (the street having previously been known as Grope Lane). When built it consisted of a large central block flanked by two two-storey wings. It was built of rough and uneven stones, which present a striking effect. There was a series of exercise yards to the rear, the whole being surrounded by a high brick wall.

This gaol was only in use for a short while, for it was closed as a result of the Prisons Act of 1877. The City Corporation then purchased the building and site for £1,750. The north-western wing and the central portion became the city police station and the south-eastern wing was converted into a fire-engine house. Further demolition led to the construction of a new road with police houses joining Gaol Street to Bath Street, which was called Delacy Street. Although this new street

The old Magistrates' Court in Gaol Street.

had rows of cottages on both sides it did not last long, for the cottages, the south-eastern wing of the original building and the fire-engine house were all demolished and a new police station was built in 1976 facing onto Bath Street. Delacy Street has since totally disappeared. The old police station survived to become the City Magistrates' Court, a use that continued till the end of the twentieth century. It was in October 2002 that, following the granting of planning and listed building consent, the building had yet another change of use – it became the Elim Pentecostal Church, the old Court One being used for services. The Elim Church has since moved to new buildings in Union Walk and the old Gaol Building is again (2018) up for sale.

37. Green Dragon Hotel, Broad Street

Formerly called the White Lion, the Green Dragon is the largest hotel in the centre of Hereford. Its early history is shrouded in mystery, but by the seventeenth century it was a typically small inn that was then owned by the College of Vicars' Choral. They sold it in 1843 and, together with adjoining properties, the inn was bought by the Bosley family. They built the large assembly room in 1845 and, in 1857 erected the Italianate front that still graces Broad Street. By that time the Green Dragon was the principal hotel in the city, stretching through to Aubrey Street at the rear. Although there was a rear access to the hotel yard, reflecting its importance, coaches could arrive at the front and drive straight through the

Above: The Green Dragon Hotel is central to Broad Steet.

Left: The Judges Room in the Green Dragon Hotel.

building. This was where the main entrance is now, with the original front door being central to the triangular pediment.

The hotel was enlarged in the early 1880s, after which it had fifty bedrooms, and again in 1913 adding a further forty bedrooms. At the beginning of the twentieth century it was advertised as having electric light throughout and a 'perfect sanitation'!

On 1 September 1928 the Green Dragon took a full-page advertisement in the *Hereford Times*. Describing itself as the 'Premier Hotel of the Wye Valley', the occasion was the completion of its new dining room, servery, kitchens, sculleries, still room, pantry and other facilities at a cost of some £12,000. The management proudly described the dining room as 'the finest dining room between Birmingham and Bristol'. The Green Dragon expanded again in 1930, purchasing the two properties to the north. Within this the panelled Judge's Room has a plasterwork ceiling with pendants and a chamfered stone fireplace with a carved lintel. The classical frontage was continued across the new additions without any apparent break.

38. Library and Museum, Broad Street

It was in 1871, when a penny rate in the city produced only £325, that James Rankin of Bryngwyn House came to the fore. Acting through the Woolhope Club (the Herefordshire Naturalists' Field Club), he provided the capital to purchase a site for a library and museum, providing that the Woolhope Club was given a suitable room in the building.

The new building, on the west side of Broad Street, was designed by F. R. Kempson, a local architect, who had just completed the country house for Rankin. The foundation stone was laid in 1873, with the completed building being opened in October 1874. The building contract price was £4,700, but with a final price of, £7,600, with the council and Sir James Rankin finding the rest. It was a great success and extensions were added to the rear in 1912 following a bequest from the Pulley family. Further building works took place in the 1960s and 1970s.

The style of the building is usually described as Anglicised Venetian Gothic. It has an intricate stone front of blue-grey Pontypridd sandstone and Camden ashlar dressings. It is notable for the astonishing array of flora and fauna that decorate the whole of the front elevation carved by Robert and William Clarke. Those of the ground-floor capitals represent Europe, Asia, Africa and America. A whole array of animals decorates the parapet.

Inside, there is a full-height entrance hall with stairs that lead up to the museum, which is on the second floor. The lending library occupies much of the ground floor behind the entrance hall, and within it there is a separate flight of stairs that leads up the reference department on the first floor. The Woolhope Club room, with its extensive library, is approached from the staircase in the entrance hall, and is on the first floor facing onto Broad Street. It has a stone balcony. On the staircase wall in the entrance hall are two mosaic pavements, which were excavated at the Roman town of Magnis (at Kenchester, some 3 miles west of Hereford) in the early twentieth century.

The library and museum in Broad Street was opened in 1874.

The old Working Boys' Home, Bath Street.

39. Working Boys' Home/Council Offices, Bath Street

The old Working Boys' Home consists of a collection of buildings on the north-east side of Bath Street as it curves round to join into St Owen Street.

The Working Boys' Home was founded in 1874 with help from Revd John Venn, and they rented a small house in Commercial Street. The foundation stone for the first building on the present site was laid in June 1876, with the home being opened in February 1877. It was certified as an Industrial School in November of that year for fifty boys aged eight to thirteen. Two short-term superintendents were followed in 1880 by Edward Horth, with his wife Elizabeth as matron. They stayed there for thirty-eight years, after which their son, also Edward, took over.

As the Hereford and District Working Boys' Home and Industrial School it took in orphans and other voluntary cases from boys 'in a state of destitution or

Above: The one-time Working Boys' Home is on Bath Street.

Below: Some of the inhabitants of the Working Boys' Home.

2185. W.B.H. HEREFORD. BOBBY and WOOD CART.

growing up under evil influences'. Their training included wood chopping, basket making, gardening and, later, tailoring along with general housework.

A new wing was added in 1886, which contained a schoolroom, workshops and an infirmary. The Meadows Memorial Hall (the building with the cupola) was added in 1895 following a grant from Mrs Meadows of Aylestone Hill. Following all this work the accommodation had increased to 125 pupils.

The Working Boys' Home closed in May 1932 and the buildings were taken over by the city and later the county council, when they were used for various purposes. Plans were made to use the site for a new fire station, but they were not accepted. Further plans were produced to use the site as part of the new University of Hereford, but these again fell through. An attempt was made to get the complex listed, but the application was turned down by English Heritage. The most recent application, to use the site for housing and including most of the present buildings, has been approved.

40. Royal National College for the Blind, Venns Lane

The college stands on around 6 acres of high ground some half a mile to the north-east of the city with wide views of the Wye Valley and its neighbourhood. The original buildings were erected at a cost of some £17,000 to the design of F. R. Kempson between 1877 and 1881 as a private school – the County College for Boys. When this closed it became one of the first teacher training colleges in the country, opening in 1904.

The original buildings are of Gothic design and of local red Holmer brick. The impressive entrance front, with its dominating central tower, has the unusual feature of four steep, crow-stepped gables linked by cast ironwork. The eastern wing was a schoolroom; the western one a dining hall. The headmaster's house was at the western end. The east wing was extended to the north in 1909, to the design of G. H. Jack. To the south-west are the Queen's Buildings, built as a library in 1972. On the east, a large two-storey classroom was built in the late 1970s. Across Venn's Lane are three halls of residence, built in the 1960s.

The Teachers Training College closed in 1979 and the buildings were taken over by the Royal National College for the Blind. Following this, there was an extensive modernisation of the halls of residence in the early 2000s to provide en-suite facilities for the residents, and in 2008, between the earlier halls and set back, a further residence hall, sports centre and outdoor floodlit sports pitch were built.

In 2009 the college became the home of the National Blind Art Collection, a collection of paintings, sculptures, installations and other works of art, designed to engage all the senses and to provide people who are visually impaired with greater accessibility to art.

The National College for the Blind was earlier the Teachers Training College.

In March 2012, the Royal National College for the Blind celebrated its 140th anniversary with a day of events at its campus, and a street collection in Hereford. Several of the buildings on the campus are now used by the Hereford College of Arts as a home to university-level courses.

41. Victoria Close (The Victoria Eye and Ear Hospital), Eign Street

Eign Street (not to be confused with Eign Road) is the main road leading westwards from the Inner Relief Road towards Hay-on-Wye and Brecon. Victoria Close is on the south side a short distance from the Inner Relief Road.

The first Eye and Ear Hospital was set up in 1882 in a leased property in front of the Baptist Church in Commercial Road. It became a charitable institution in 1884, serving Herefordshire, the neighbouring counties and the whole of South Wales.

Work began on the purpose-built building in Eign Street in 1888, and it opened in August of the following year. The hospital was renamed the Victoria Eye Hospital in 1923. Extensions were built in 1937 and 1966.

All the eye hospital services were moved to the County Hospital at the beginning of the twenty-first century and the old buildings were sold for a price in excess of £700,000. The site was then redeveloped for housing with the main building being converted into flats and apartments, while a further twenty-one three-storey houses were built in the grounds. It is now called Victoria Court.

Adjoining the Eye Hospital site on the west is Victoria House, which was built in 1912 as a home for the renowned eye surgeon Frances Woodley so that he

The Victoria Eye and Ear Hospital opened in 1889.

could live near to the hospital. It is a handsome Arts and Crafts building. When eye care was moved to the County Hospital, the building was taken over by the National Health Service for offices, but when they moved out, the building was left empty. A planning application to demolish the building was refused, and since 2011 it has stood empty and derelict, partly boarded up with broken windows, and now stands in the middle of what has become a public car park.

42. Library Building, Hereford Cathedral

The Library Building, which stands to the west of the cathedral, and is approached through the Bishop's Cloister, is of two periods. The earlier part, known as the Dean Leigh Library, was built in 1896–97 and is of Perpendicular style.

In 1996, a larger L-shaped extension was added to house the Hereford Mappa Mundi and the two chained libraries (the cathedral's own, and the one from All Saint's Church). It was designed by Whitfield Partners and cost around £3 million. It was opened by the Queen in 1996.

The Cathedral Chained Library contains around 1,500 books and manuscripts, which date from the eighth to the nineteenth centuries. Its book presses and reading desks were made in 1611. It is the largest in the country to survive with all

Above: The Cathedral Library building from Broad Street.

Below: The Chained Library is in the new part of the Cathedral Library building, which was opened in 1996.

its chains and locks intact. The specially designed chamber means that the whole library can now be seen, in its original seventeenth-century arrangement, for the first time for over 150 years.

For many years the Mappa Mundi hung in a glass-fronted case in the north choir aisle with relatively little recognition. In 1988, during a financial crisis, the Dean and Chapter proposed selling the Mappa. Fortunately, due to large donations from the National Heritage Memorial Fund, Paul Getty, and many members of the public, the Mappa was saved for Hereford, and the construction of the new library building followed.

The Hereford Mappa Mundi is a map of the known world that was drawn on vellum (calf skin) in great detail around 1290. It is the largest medieval map known to have survived complete. The map is circular and interpreted the world in spiritual as well as geographical terms. It includes Biblical illustrations as well as portrayals of classical learning and legends. It is generally believed that it was made in Lincoln, although there have been suggestions that it was actually made in Hereford.

East is at the top of the map; at the centre is Jerusalem – the centre of the Christian world. Drawings on the map include elephants, camels and lions as well as mythical beasts. The top of the map shows Christ sitting at the Day of Judgement, flanked by angels.

43. Barr's Court Railway Station, Commercial Road

Hereford was the last town of comparable size to be connected to the railway network. Barr's Court station takes its name from the earlier temporary station opened in October 1853 and located opposite Barr's Court to the north of the present station and east of the canal basin of the Hereford and Gloucester Canal, opened in May 1845. Designed by John Penson, architect, Barr's Court was a terminal station for the standard gauge (4 foot 8.5 inches) Shrewsbury & Hereford Railway and the broad gauge (7 foot 0.25 inches) Hereford, Ross and Gloucester Railway. The design was described as Tudor or Elizabethan; today it is described as Gothic Revival. It was completed in 1856 at a cost of £6,788 14 s 8d. In 1878 Barr's Court was redeveloped by making it a through station with island platforms.

Barton station, to the west of the city and close to where Sainsbury's supermarket now stands, opened in 1853 for the Newport Abergavenny and Hereford Railway. It was closed to the majority of passenger services to the south, which were then passed through Barr's Court by means of a loop line opened in 1893. The final development at Barr's Court was the inclusion of a bay platform for the Hereford, Hay and Brecon Railway, following the closure of their Moorfield's station in 1893. The line from Hereford to Brecon via Hay-on-Wye was closed on 31 December 1962, and the one to Gloucester followed on 2 November 1964 – both victims of

Barr's Court railway station was opened in 1856.

An early photograph of Barr's Court railway station.

the Beeching Report and Minister of Transport White Paper. In 1973 Barr's Court station was included in the statuary list of Buildings of Special Architectural or Historic Interest.

The area in front of Barr's Court station has changed significantly in the last few years with the construction of the Hereford Inner Link Road and large car-parking areas. The whole area is set to become the transport centre for Hereford for the foreseeable future.

44. Town Hall, St Owen Street

Hereford Town Hall stands on the south side of St Owen Street, a short distance from St Peter's Square. It was built in 1902–04 to the design of Harry A. Cheers. It is typical of its period, the façade being of biscuit-coloured terracotta in a Jacobean baroque style. Previously the city council had met in several places, including the Tolsey (then at the High Town end of Commercial Street), and in the old Market Hall, which stood in the centre of High Town until its demolition in 1861. It then met in the Guildhall, which was accessed from Widemarsh Street, while the offices and Mayor's Parlour were in the Mansion House (see No. 19).

The new Town Hall replaced a row of small cottages, which were owned by the daughters of a former town clerk. The foundation stone was laid on 13 May 1902 by Princess Henry of Battenberg and opened on 9 June 1904. She was the youngest of the nine children of Queen Victoria and was born in 1857, when she was known as Princess Beatrice. In 1885 she married Prince Henry of Battenberg, who was then made a British citizen. They had four children, but he died of malaria on an expedition to West Africa in 1895. During the First World War, when the royal family strove to disassociate itself from its German roots, Princess Henry reverted to her original title of HRH Princess Beatrice.

The Town Hall was the headquarters of the Hereford City Council until 1998 when the Herefordshire Council was founded, replacing the earlier Hereford and Worcester County Council. It was at that time that the city lost its status and became a parish council, but it retained its right to have a mayor. Although its powers are limited, by royal charter it is still called the city council and has responsibilities for looking after the historic silver plate, ceremonial robes, etc. Recently the new Hereford Civic Museum was opened upstairs in the Town Hall next to the Mayor's Parlour and exhibits the charters, which date back to 1189, and most of the silver plate.

The Town Hall is a Grade II* listed building. The entrance hall, the splendid Empire staircase, the Great Hall, and the Council Chamber are of particular note. At the rear is the Hereford Registry Office and the Town Hall is now regularly used for wedding receptions.

The Town Hall, which replaced a row of cottages, was opened in 1904.

Hereford Civic Museum in the Town Hall.

45. Lichfield Vaults, Church Street

Church Street (or Cabbage Lane as it was long known, before becoming the more pretentious Capuchin Lane – named after the Order of Friars Minor Capuchin) is the narrow street that joins High Town and the Cathedral Close. It has always had a wide variety of shops and in its time has been the home of several small inns. The Lichfield Vaults and the Grapes (see No. 15) are the only survivors.

   The origin of the Lichfield Vaults is shrouded in mystery, but there was certainly a tavern here towards the end of the eighteenh century and probably earlier. It was then called The Dog, and James Allen was landlord in 1793. It was very small and L-shaped, but it was eventually merged with the adjoining building. The name was changed by 1885 when the inn was taken over by the Lichfield Brewery Co., founded in Lichfield, Staffordshire, in 1869.

   In the early twentieth century the public area was minute: the public bar was just 8 feet long by 5 feet wide – smaller than a prison cell, and inevitably it was standing room only! At the rear there was an L-shaped smoke room with wall-seating and two fireplaces. Radical alterations in 1914 resulted in the amalgamation of

The Lichfield Vaults inn is in Church Street.

Inside the Lichfield Vaults inn.

bar and smoke room into one large room, but with a screen between the two parts – the proprieties were preserved and the separation between workmen and tradesmen was to continue for some time. Even now, there is still some separation between the front and rear public areas.

In the mid-1930s the Lichfield Brewery Co. was eventually taken over by Allsops and then by Ind Coope. At some time after the Second World War, possibly in 1949, the pub was again radically altered. The central stack was totally removed and a new fireplace and chimney stack was built against the north wall, and the southern side passage was incorporated into the building. The work was completed when the whole Church Street façade was rebuilt. Three tenements at the rear were also demolished to provide the inn with a secluded garden area.

46. No. 13 Bridge Street (Crystal Rooms)

The art deco façade of what was known at different times as Franklin Barnes and the Crystal Rooms is on the east side of Bridge Street.

The site has had a complex history. In the eighteenth century it was occupied by the Royal Oak Inn, which had stables stretching back to Gwynne Street. In 1867 the Alhambra Music Hall and Palace of Amusement opened at the rear of the inn, presumably replacing the stables. The Royal Oak closed around 1879, but the

Alhambra continued in use. By 1891 the old Royal Oak had become the premises of Rogers and Co., Seed and Corn Merchants, but by 1912, the building had been taken over by Franklin Barnes and Co., who also made use of the old Alhambra as a seed warehouse.

In 1936 the theatre and the old Royal Oak were demolished to make way for larger premises for Franklin Barnes. The site was developed in a revolutionary way including a steel-framed structure with curtain walls. It stretched back to Gwynne Street and included the 1880s Gwynne Street warehouse. There was a square, arched entry to the rear courtyard. The design, by Bettington and Co., included the art deco façade in the form of 'decorative modernist'. It has Vitrolite cladding in green and primrose, as had been first used in the *Daily Express* building in London's Fleet Street.

The new building continued in use until the 1960s, but eventually Franklin Barnes moved to premises at the corner of Commercial Road and Blueschool Street, and the Bridge Street buildings became the Crystal Rooms Nightclub. Famously known as 'sticky carpets', it was the 'Naughty but Nice' Friday club night that put Hereford on the underground music map.

The Crystal Rooms site was sold in 2004, and the rear buildings were all demolished, leaving the art deco front standing and still looking good at the present day. A large apartment block has developed in Gwynne Street, with a narrow entrance passage through the northern end of the Bridge Street façade.

A late nineteenth-century engraving of No. 13 Bridge Street, from Gwynne Street.

The art deco design of No. 13 Bridge Street.

47. Tesco, Bewell Street

The Tesco supermarket was built in the 1980s on a large car park that surrounded the then disused mid-eighteenth-century Bewell House, situated in the north-western corner of the medieval walled city. The superstore was built shortly after the construction of the A49 Inner Relief Road, which skirts the site on the west.

Prior to being used as a car park, the part of the site to the east of Bewell House, had, for many years, been occupied by the Imperial Brewery, run by the Watkins family during the nineteenth and early twentieth centuries; first by Charles, a local entrepreneur, followed by his son, Alfred (see No. 13).

When the Inner Relief Road was built it cut slightly across the line of the medieval city wall, which had been demolished many years previously. As part of the construction of the Tesco supermarket it was decided to once again provide the sense of enclosure that the medieval wall had given, by facing the new building with sandstone laid similarly to the lost medieval wall. A plaque, set into the real line of the wall to the east of the fake wall by the pedestrian entry from New Market Street, records the relief road construction. The original line of the medieval defences is recorded in a rather unusual way. On the roundabout to the north-west of the supermarket is a depression that is on the line of the ditch that ran on the outside of the medieval wall. Until recently this depression was, rather appropriately, accompanied with a weeping willow tree.

The entrance to the supermarket's underground car park, which includes the area of the old brewery cellars, runs from the Inner Relief Road in front of the Grade II* listed Bewell House, which is now used as offices.

Above: The Bewell
Street frontage of
the Tesco store.

Left: The Imperial
Brewery in Bewell
Street in the
nineteenth century.

Bewell House.

48. The Courtyard Theatre, Edgar Street

Following the demolition of the Kemble Theatre in 1963 and the closure of the Regal (formerly the Palladium in Berrington Street), the Garrick Theatre, in Widemarsh Street, long used as the county library, could have been reused as a theatre, but this was demolished in 1978. Herefordshire was then without any real theatre.

In the late 1970s, the municipal swimming baths in Edgar Street were closed and replaced with a new building south of the River Wye. Various local societies then got together and embarked on a scheme to convert the old baths into a theatre. A charitable trust was set up and an appeal launched, and finally the conversion work went ahead. A sloping floor, created for the raked seating for 350 seats, and a stage 30 feet wide and 24 feet deep was built. The building included dressing rooms, a bar and a restaurant. It was in 1979 that the former baths reopened as the Nell Gwynne Theatre and Arts Centre. Although films were added to the programme and many volunteers helped with the bar and restaurant, it became insolvent in 1984 and closed. It reopened in the following year with funding from the city council, but problems continued and by the 1990s it became apparent that the fabric of the building was in very poor condition.

The solution was radical: demolish the present building and build a new theatre. An application to the National Lottery (one of the first such applications in the region) for £3.75 million was successful. The competition for designing the new building was won by Birmingham architect Glenn Howells.

Above: The Swimming Baths converted into the New Hereford Theatre.

Below: The Courtyard Theatre.

The new, modern building – the Courtyard Centre for the Arts – opened in September 1998 and has continued successfully from that time. It contains a theatre seating 434 and a smaller studio seating 126. The spacious foyer with bar and restaurant areas is well appreciated by theatregoers.

49. Left Bank Village, Gwynne Street and Bridge Street

The Village is situated on the north bank of the River Wye, on the eastern side of Bridge Street and to the south of Gwynne Street (named after Nell Gwynne, the mistress of Charles II, who was reputedly born there in 1650). Before the new development, the western part of the site was occupied by Nos 20–22 Bridge Street, while to the east was Gwynne House and its grounds, including a coach house and stable block. The grounds are surrounded by the Bishop's Palace gardens to the north and east. The new development was on the Bridge Street frontage, and the Gwynne House complex survives.

The site facing onto Bridge Street and south of Gwynne Street included, during the nineteenth century, the Bell Inn on the south side of Gwynne Street – the headquarters of the bargees on the River Wye for many years. In the latter part of the twentieth century the buildings facing onto Bridge Street were the premises of Mead and Tomkinson.

The old riverside warehouse is now part of the Left Bank Village.

Gwynne House on the north side of the Left Bank Village courtyard.

The riverside frontage of the Left Bank Village.

At the end of the twentieth century the whole of the site was acquired by Eign Enterprises Ltd and all the buildings facing Bridge Street were demolished to make way for the new development. At the time it was described in the *Hereford Times* as 'the biggest single private development ever undertaken in Hereford'. The new restaurant, conference centre and shops complex was designed by Jamieson Associates and opened in July 2000 with a champagne reception. It was the brainchild of Dr and Mrs Heijn, who invested several million pounds in the project. The three-storey stepped terraces overlooking the Wye are a notable feature.

Gwynne House is a brick building of the late eighteenth century with a nineteenth-century veranda. It now contains three luxury self-contained apartments, used mainly as wedding accommodation. The old stable block to the east is used for meetings.

50. The Old Market, Newmarket Street

The Old Market sits on the north side of Newmarket Street and to the east of Edgar Street (the A49 trunk road). The rather odd juxtaposition of names reflects the history of the site, for before this development the whole area was the Hereford Livestock Market. It was opened on 17 October 1856, and from that time the market ceased to be in the streets, although cattle and sheep still arrived on the hoof.

The market was of considerable importance and by 1900 over 150,000 animals passed through each year. There was even a rail line, constructed in 1914, which crossed Edgar Street. The market was enlarged in 1956 with new buildings and the Langford Sale Ring. The Inner Relief Road, completed in 1966, allowed for further building work on the 12.5-acre site. After this the animal throughput rose to over 440,000.

Almost all was demolished, and the new £90 million development, now well known as the Old Market, was opened on 1 May 2014 with a supermarket, eighteen retail units, eight restaurants and a six-screen cinema. There are some 600 car-parking spaces, and various open public spaces. Recently, Historic England's Urban Panel visited the site and praised how Herefordshire Council had successfully managed to integrate modern developments, such as this, with the city's historic core.

One building survives from the Livestock Market days and even earlier. Built in 1812 as a private house for Charles Heather, it was used for a short while as the Hereford Improvement Office, before becoming the New Market Tavern. In 1857 a concert room was added to the building and the whole was then advertised as the New Cattle Market Hotel. This building is now a Zizzi restaurant.

Above: The Widemarsh Street entry into the Old Market.

Below: An internal street view in the Old Market.

Acknowledgements

We wish to thank the following for permission to take photographs: Hereford Cathedral Chapter (Cathedral, Vicars' Choral College, Nos 1 and 11); Right Revd Richard Frith, Bishop of Hereford (Bishops Palace, No. 3); Revd Andy Morgan (St Peter's Church, No. 4); Preb. Revd Rob North and Jackie Munford (All Saints Church, No. 5); Hereford Cathedral Chapter, Dr Rosemary Firman and Sarah Arrowsmith (Cathedral Barn, Cathedral Library, Nos 6 and 42); John Eisel (Castle Cliffe, No. 7); Pete Edwards (Black Lion Inn, No. 14); Martin Pearson (The Cosy Club, Widemarsh Street, No. 17); Judy Stevenson and Julia Radburn (Herefordshire Council, for The Old House, Museum and Library, Nos 18 and 38); the late Mark Black (The Mansion House, No. 19); Peter Amor (The Barrels, No. 21); George Watkins (Castle House Hotel, No. 22); Canon Dr Howard Tomlinson, Paul Smith (Hereford Cathedral School buildings, Nos 9, 13 and 27); Father Michael Evans (St Francis Xavier Church, No. 33); Sharon Davis (Green Dragon Hotel, No. 37); Hereford City Council (Town Hall, No. 44); Andy Loizou (Lichfield Vaults, No. 45); Frank Bennett (Working Boys' Home, No. 39); and Dr Philip Cartwright, Julie Phillips and Ron Pensom for helping to correct the text.

Main Books Consulted

Brooks, Alan and Nikolaus Pevsner, *The Buildings of England: Herefordshire* (Yale University Press, 2012)

Eisel, John, *Woolhope Naturalists Field Club*, Vol. 57 (2009)

Eisel, John, *Woolhope Naturalists Field Club*, Vol. 59 (2013)

Eisel, John, *Woolhope Naturalists Field Club*, Vol. 61 (2015)

Foxton, Derek, *Hereford in Old Picture Postcards*

Foxton, Derek, *Hereford Then and Now*, Vols 1, 2 and 3

Grist, Betty and Derek Foxton, *Edwardian Hereford* (1993)

Haig, Robert, *A History of Theatres and Performers in Herefordshire* (Logaston Press, 2002)

Johnson, Andy and Ron Shoesmith (eds), *The Story of Hereford* (Logaston Press, 2016)

O'Donnell, Jean, *The Rev. John Venn and the Friends of Hereford Poor* (Logaston Press, 2007)

Shoesmith, Ron, *Hereford, History and Guide* (Allen Sutton Publishing, 1992)

Shoesmith, Ron and Jennifer Shoesmith, *Alfred Watkins' Herefordshire* (Logaston Press, 2012)

Shoesmith, Ron and John Eisel, *The Pubs of Hereford City* (Logaston Press, 2004)

Wood, Gordon, *Railways of Hereford* (Kidderminster Railway Museum, 2003)

About the Authors

Ron Shoesmith

Ron came to Hereford in 1962 to run a youth hostel at Staunton-on-Wye. He became increasingly interested in archaeology and in 1974 helped set up the City of Hereford Archaeology Committee, of which he became Director of Excavations. He continued in that role for twenty-one years, conducting many excavations in Herefordshire and neighbouring counties. He is a fellow of the Society of Antiquaries of London and has written several books on Herefordshire's history and archaeology.

Derek Foxton

Derek has lived in Hereford for very nearly all his life. Educated in the city and county, he graduated in dentistry at London University in 1964. After running a multi-surgery practice for thirty-five years, he retired and concentrated on his hobbies. A collection of Hereford photographs, postcards and books were accumulated over these years and have been the source for several books. He also has a collection of very early motor vehicles.